THE 10 GROSSEST ANIMALS

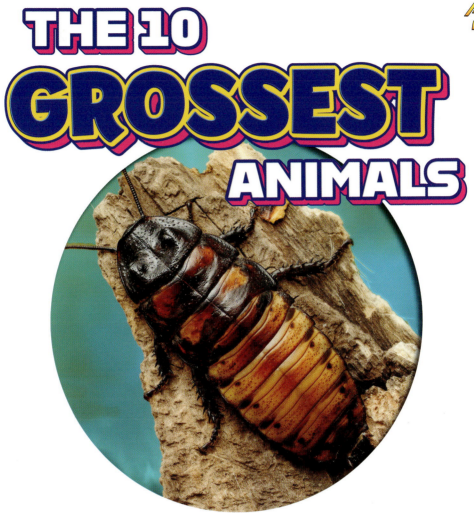

BY RACHEL ROSE

Minneapolis, Minnesota

Credits

Cover and title page, © EcoPic/iStock, © torook/Shutterstock, and © lersan8910/iStock; Title Page, © torook/Shutterstock; 4, © Yü Lan/Adobe Stock Photos; 5, © Phichaklim1/iStock; 6, © Nature Picture Library/Alamy Stock Photo; 7, © blickwinkel/Alamy Stock Photo; 8, © robertharding/Alamy Stock Photo; 8–9, © EcoPic/Getty Images; 10, © JeremyRichards/iStock; 11, © David Osborn/Alamy Stock Photo; 12, © Chronicle/Alamy Stock Photo; 12–13, © Avalon.red/Alamy Stock Photo; 14, © Joe McDonald/Shutterstock; 15, © John Cancalosi/Alamy Stock Photo; 16, © National Oceanic and Atmospheric Administration/Wikimedia Commons; 16–17, © Josh/Adobe Stock Photos; 18, © Mendez, Raymond/Animals Animals; 18–19, © Neil Bromhall/Nature Picture Library; 20, © ffennema/Getty Images; 20–21, © Brandon Cole Marine Photography/Alamy Stock Photo; 22T, © Cay-Uwe/iStock; 22M, © Vitalii Puzankov/iStock; 22B, © Kateryna Kukota/iStock; 23, © strikerx98/iStock.

Bearport Publishing Company Product Development Team

Publisher: Jen Jenson; Director of Product Development: Spencer Brinker; Managing Editor: Allison Juda; Editor: Cole Nelson; Associate Editor: Naomi Reich; Associate Editor: Tiana Tran; Art Director: Colin O'Dea; Designer: Kim Jones; Designer: Kayla Eggert; Product Development Specialist: Owen Hamlin

Statement on Usage of Generative Artificial Intelligence

Bearport Publishing remains committed to publishing high-quality nonfiction books. Therefore, we restrict the use of generative AI to ensure accuracy of all text and visual components pertaining to a book's subject. See BearportPublishing.com for details.

Library of Congress Cataloging-in-Publication Data is available at www.loc.gov or upon request from the publisher.

ISBN: 979-8-89232-640-7 (hardcover)
ISBN: 979-8-89232-689-6 (ebook)

Copyright © 2025 Bearport Publishing Company. All rights reserved. No part of this publication may be reproduced in whole or in part, stored in any retrieval system, or transmitted in any form or by any means, electronic, mechanical, photocopying, recording, or otherwise, without written permission from the publisher.

For more information, write to Bearport Publishing, 5357 Penn Avenue South, Minneapolis, MN 55419.

CONTENTS

Grossest of the Gross.............................4

#10 House Fly..............................5

#9 Purple Frog............................6

#8 Madagascar Hissing Cockroach...........7

#7 Warthog...............................8

#6 Elephant Seal.........................10

#5 Vampire Bat..........................12

#4 Regal Horned Lizard..................14

#3 Blobfish.............................16

#2 Naked Mole Rat.......................18

#1 Hagfish..............................20

Even More Gross Animals.......................22

Glossary.....................................23

Index..24

Read More....................................24

Learn More Online............................24

About the Author.............................24

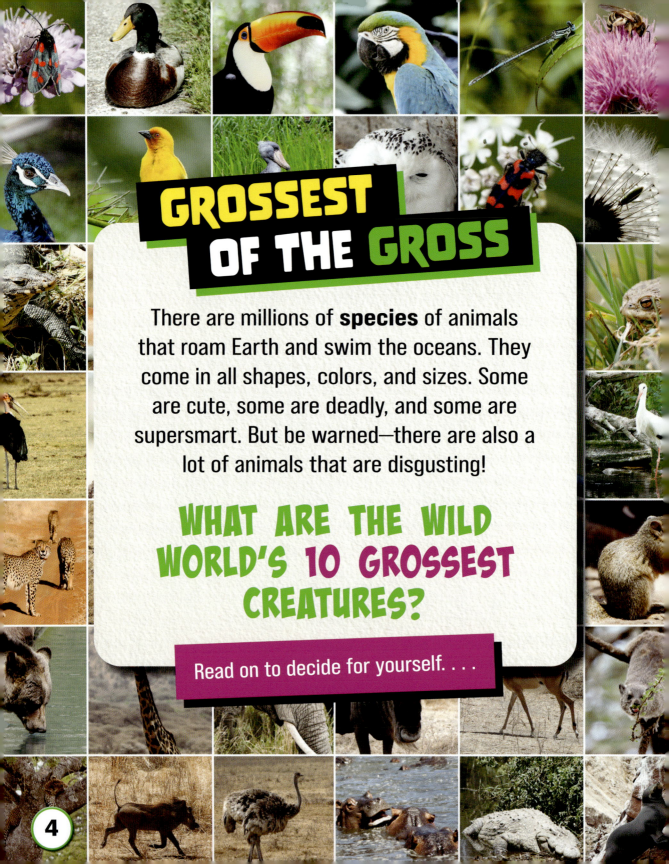

GROSSEST OF THE GROSS

There are millions of **species** of animals that roam Earth and swim the oceans. They come in all shapes, colors, and sizes. Some are cute, some are deadly, and some are supersmart. But be warned—there are also a lot of animals that are disgusting!

WHAT ARE THE WILD WORLD'S 10 GROSSEST CREATURES?

Read on to decide for yourself. . . .

#10 HOUSE FLY

Be careful of what you eat, especially when a house fly lands on your food. This insect can't chew, so it has a gross way of preparing its meal. The fly spits out saliva on its lunch, turning solid food into liquid. Then, this buzzing insect slurps up its runny meal. *Yuck!*

This insect can spread **diseases** among humans.

Flies can taste with their toes!

Flies sometimes poop on your food, too!

#9 PURPLE FROG

Oink! A pointed **snout** gives this creature the name pig-nosed frog, but that's the only pig-like thing about it. The purple frog's puffed-up body looks more like a lump of flesh. Unlike other frogs, this purple blob can't jump high because of its short legs. Instead, the slimy-looking creature uses its stumpy legs to dig underground.

Purple frogs **burrow** underground for insects and termites.

Some people say purple frogs look like turtles without shells.

This frog may look like a pig, but its mating call sounds like a chicken.

#8 MADAGASCAR HISSING COCKROACH

Hiss! Was that a snake? Nope, it was the Madagascar hissing cockroach. Not only is this insect the biggest kind of roach, it's also the loudest. The shiny cockroach's hiss can be heard from 12 feet (4 m) away. This sound comes from holes on the sides of its creepy-crawly body.

Male hissing cockroaches have large horns.

These cockroaches can grow up to 4 inches (10 cm) long!

Hissing keeps **predators**, such as birds and snakes, away.

#7 WARTHOG

That's no beauty mark! Warthogs are named for the wartlike bumps on their faces. These lumps are not actually warts but rather thick growths of skin. And they can get big—up to 6 in. (15 cm) long. That's about the size of a dollar bill! Males have three pairs of bumps close to their eyes, snouts, and jaws. Females have only two pairs.

Rolling around in the mud protects a warthog's skin from the sun.

These hogs are peaceful creatures. They typically run away rather than fight.

Warthogs use their wartlike bumps and curved tusks for defense.

Warthogs can run as fast as 35 miles per hour (56 kph).

#6 ELEPHANT SEAL

Get a load of that nose! Elephant seals are named for their huge, lumpy, trunk-like noses. Their honkers can grow more than 2 ft. (0.6 m) long! During mating season, the odd schnozzes get even bigger. Male elephant seals **inflate** their large noses to make loud roars. The sound shows off their strength and keeps other males away. Stay back!

Elephant seals don't have earflaps—just holes in the sides of their heads.

Males can weigh up to 5,000 pounds (2,200 kg). That's heavier than some pickup trucks.

These seals can hold their breath underwater for more than an hour.

They shed large patches of body hair once a year.

Male seals are called bulls. Females are cows.

#5 VAMPIRE BAT

As their name suggests, vampire bats are out for blood. These flying **mammals** feast on animal blood. First, they cut their prey with sharp little teeth. Then, they lap up the oozing liquid as it spills from the wound. When there isn't enough food to go around, vampire bats will sometimes spit up a bloody meal to share with another hungry bat.

Vampire bats drink mostly the blood of cows, pigs, and horses.

#4 REGAL HORNED LIZARD

Splat! The regal horned lizard is armed for survival with a pretty nasty way to scare off predators. These lizards can shoot out a stream of blood—from their eyes! Using perfect aim, these regal reptiles squirt the red stuff directly into their predators' mouths. Now, that's a nice shot!

They can change color to **blend** in with their desert surroundings.

Horned lizards can also puff up like balloons to scare predators away.

These lizards get their name from the crown-like horns on their heads.

They can shoot blood up to 4 ft. (1 m) away.

#3 BLOBFISH

The blobfish is often called the ugliest creature on Earth. That's because we've seen its floppy, frowning face most frequently out of its natural, deepwater **habitat**. This odd-looking fish is usually found near the ocean floor. When pulled out of the water, the blobfish flattens into a mushy pile of goo. Throw the blob back in!

The high **pressure** of the water at the ocean floor holds the blobfish's body together.

#2 NAKED MOLE RAT

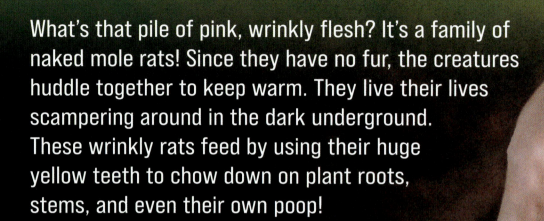

What's that pile of pink, wrinkly flesh? It's a family of naked mole rats! Since they have no fur, the creatures huddle together to keep warm. They live their lives scampering around in the dark underground. These wrinkly rats feed by using their huge yellow teeth to chow down on plant roots, stems, and even their own poop!

These rats can dig tunnels as deep as 7 ft. (2 m).

19

#1 HAGFISH

A hagfish is disgusting! When it's hungry, this slimy, snakelike creature slithers into the body of a dead animal—eating it from the inside out. To escape predators, the fish covers itself in lots of slime. Sometimes, it even sneezes the gooey stuff out from the **nostril** on the top of its head. *Gross!*

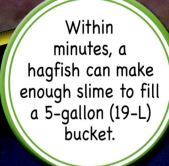

Within minutes, a hagfish can make enough slime to fill a 5-gallon (19-L) bucket.

EVEN MORE GROSS ANIMALS

These 10 animals aren't the only creepy ones in the wild. What are some other gross creatures?

TURKEY VULTURE
Turkey vultures can't sweat, so they keep themselves cool by peeing and pooping on their legs.

LEECH
These slimy, blood-sucking worms latch onto their prey. Some leeches can eat several times their own weight in blood.

HONEY BADGER
Don't be fooled by the name. Honey badgers are anything but sweet. They can squirt out a foul-smelling liquid from their butts. *Pee-yew!*

GLOSSARY

blend to mix in with

burrow to make a hole or tunnel

diseases illnesses or sicknesses

habitat a place in nature where an animal or plant normally lives

inflate to fill up with air

mammals warm-blooded animals that have hair and feed their young milk from their bodies

muscles parts of the body that make it move

nostril an opening in the nose that is used for breathing and smelling

predators animals that hunt and kill other animals for food

pressure the force of pressing on something

snout the nose and mouth of an animal

species groups that animals are divided into, according to similar characteristics

INDEX

blood 12–15, 22
diseases 5
female 8, 11
flesh 6, 18
habitat 16
male 7–8, 10–11
muscles 17, 19
nose 6, 10–11
nostril 20
ocean 4, 16
poop 5, 18, 22
predators 7, 14, 20
slime 20
snout 6, 8
warts 8

READ MORE

Kaiser, Brianna. *Weird Animals. (Wonderfully Weird).* Minneapolis: Lerner Publications, 2024.

Ruby, Rex. *Bloody Eyes: Gross Horned Lizards (Amazing Animal Self-Defense).* Minneapolis: Bearport Publishing Company, 2023.

LEARN MORE ONLINE

1. Go to **FactSurfer.com** or scan the QR code below.
2. Enter "**10 Grossest Animals**" into the search box.
3. Click on the cover of this book to see a list of websites.

ABOUT THE AUTHOR

Rachel Rose writes books for kids and teaches yoga. Her favorite animal for all time is her dog, Sandy.